Let Me Sow Love

D1052472

Let Me Sow Love

Living the Peace Prayer of St. Francis

James E. Adams

ave maria press   Notre Dame, Indiana

© 2003 by Creative Communications for the Parish, Inc.

www.avemariapress.com

International Standard Book Number: 0-87793-989-6

Cover and text design by Brian C. Conley

Printed and bound in the United States of America.

Library of Congress Cataloging-in-Publication Data
Adams, James E., 1946-
  Let me sow love : living the peace prayer of St. Francis /
James E. Adams.
      p. cm.
  ISBN 0-87793-989-6
  1. Prayer of St. Francis of Assisi. 2. Christian life--Catholic
authors. 3. Prayer--Catholic Church. I. Title.

BV284.P73 A33 2003
242'.7--dc21

                                                    2002152564
                                                            CIP

"A Simple Prayer"

Lord, make me an instrument of your peace.
Where there is hatred, let me sow love;
where there is injury, pardon;
where there is doubt, faith;
where there is despair, hope;
where there is darkness, light;
and where there is sadness, joy.
O Divine Master,
grant that I may not so much seek
to be consoled as to console;
to be understood as to understand;
to be loved as to love.
For it is in giving that we receive;
it is in pardoning that we are pardoned;
and it is in dying that we are born
to eternal life.

Contents

Introduction

My main goal in publishing these reflections is to help you, the reader, renew your commitment to personal prayer and to gospel holiness through a deeper appreciation of the Peace Prayer of St. Francis, or as it is now called at Franciscan sites in Assisi, "A Simple Prayer."

This is an ambitious goal for which I claim no special qualifications. Indeed, I'm counting as much on the resources readers will bring to their reading of this book as on my qualifications as a writer on spiritual topics. In your faith-filled reading, what I'm anticipating is the help of the Holy Spirit.

Yet after more than seventeen years as editor of *Living Faith: Daily Catholic Devotions*, I hope I have learned something about what can be helpful to Catholics for their prayer. *Living Faith* provides brief personal reflections from a variety of Catholic contributors on themes from the daily Mass scripture readings.

In the earliest years, I felt apologetic that the reflections weren't longer, more exhaustive, and "official." Gradually I began to realize that *Living Faith* reflections are helpful to so many not *despite* their brevity but rather *because* they are a brief, pointed, and personal sharing of insights and experiences by Catholics about everyday difficulties and achievements in their prayer lives.

So my alerting you here that these reflections are my own brief and personal (perhaps even idiosyncratic) reactions to the words, concepts, and sentiments of the Peace Prayer isn't an apology. Rather, it's an explanation so you know what to expect. If you are to be disappointed (and I don't think you will be), I'd prefer you be disappointed with what I've written rather than disappointed by my failure to write what you expected.

"A Simple Prayer" or "The Peace Prayer" linked to St. Francis has become one of the most popular prayers of Christians of many traditions. French author Christian Renoux, in a recently-published book, reports that the prayer was first published in a newspaper in Normandy, France, in 1912. Renoux says some parts of the prayer have elements traced back to William the Conqueror's chaplain. So the origins of the prayer may go back to the late eleventh century.

The then-newly published Peace Prayer became popular in Europe during and after World War I. A French delegation took a copy of the prayer to Rome and presented it to Pope Benedict XV. Later it was published in *L'Osservatore Romano*. The prayer is said to have gained wide circulation in the United States in part because an American seminarian (later to be a famous Cardinal Archbishop) Francis Spellman, who studied in Rome at the time the prayer was becoming known there, used it on a holy card for his first Mass.

Rare is the collection of favorite Catholic prayers published in the last seventy-five years that does not include the Peace Prayer. Its aspirations, if not the words themselves, have found their way into many popular contemporary hymns.

"Artists and musicians have vied with one another in popularizing" the Peace Prayer, Msgr. Charles J. Dollen writes in *Traditional Catholic Prayers*, noting also that the prayer "has an ecumenical appeal that makes it spring lightly to the lips of all."

In short, the Peace Prayer has become a fixture in popular Christianity, a part of the cultural background of Christianity in our time. Reflecting on it is surely worthwhile for any Christian of our time.

We know the prayer in its final form wasn't composed by St. Francis, but scholars seem to agree that we can describe it as *inspired* by Francis and strongly influenced by the Franciscan spiritual tradition.

Need anything be said here about St. Francis? Indeed, *can* anything new be said about the saint whose universal reputation was once so aptly summarized by biographer Raphael Brown as "the most faithful follower and perfect imitator of Jesus Christ the world has ever seen"?

Francis (1182-1226) was born into a prosperous Italian family. Impulsively romantic, he was first attracted to a life of adventure, going off to war when he was about twenty years old. He was captured and spent a year in prison. Returning home very ill, he suffered through a long recovery during which he underwent a conversion to Christ. He began serving lepers, the very sight of whom previously had repulsed him. His life of poverty and service in imitation of Christ began attracting others. He called his community of begging preachers the "Friars Minor," or "Little Brothers." Francis was noted for the joy and selflessness with which he embraced other fellow creatures and, ultimately, all of reality, including death.

Some aspects of St. Francis's life and spirituality are easy for us to identify with, but there is enough of a cultural divide between his era and ours that it is necessary to try to understand St. Francis's mentality so as better to understand some Peace Prayer themes. However, my intention isn't to train you to pray the Peace Prayer in exactly the same way that the saint from the Middle Ages after whom it's named might have prayed it. That is not possible or desirable. Rather, the goal is to help you pray it with a devotion genuinely your own, shaped by the fundamentals of current Catholic spirituality and that of recent generations.

In this book I also share some thoughts on prayer in general, and I frequently make use of elements in the Peace Prayer to help elucidate the process of prayer generally. Precisely how one prays or what words, concepts, and sentiments one uses in prayer are significant, like the wheels that help the aircraft take off. Once airborne the wheels need to be tucked up and out of the way so they don't impede flight. In that sense, the words, concepts, and sentiments of particular prayers are secondary in the act of praying.

Discussion of prayer in general is helpful, I think, because we take so much for granted about prayer, and we tend to forget the basics. I was almost startled recently by a passage in the *Catechism* reminding me that the three basic religious *duties* I am to fulfill if I am to call myself a Catholic are prayer, fasting, and almsgiving. Prayer is among my *personal* religious duties. No one can do it for me. Not only is the Christian to fast and give alms *in secret*, "but when you pray, go to your inner room, close the door, and pray to your Father *in secret*" (Mt 6:6 NAB). I emphasize the word because, surely, one of the implications of "praying in secret" is that we can't fall back on words, concepts, and sentiments that aren't at least minimally our own.

Because prayer is a personal religious duty, we must *personalize* it if we are to pray with a minimum of fervor and devotion. That doesn't mean we have to compose our own prayers. But surely it is helpful, if not essential, for us to understand the nuances of prayers we use, and to try to make our own the words, concepts, and sentiments of those prayers.

Why unpack, reflect on, and analyze the words of a simple prayer steeped in self-giving love and concern for others? Don't these words either flow freely from our lips and so function prayerfully—or they do not flow freely? And if the words do not flow freely, would we be better to abandon those particular words entirely? Yes, if we are talking about the act of praying itself. We cannot be analyzing, making the words, concepts, and sentiments our own, *as* we pray. We would be tongue-tied, stuttering over the very words, concepts, and sentiments that were supposed to help us. That would be like trying to learn the language of traffic signals and signs *while* driving.

What I'm offering here is *preparation before prayer* in the hope that you will learn to use this particular prayer as astutely, generously, and wholeheartedly as you can.

What are we really asking for in this prayer? What is "peace" anyway? When we use "peace" and "love" in this prayer, are we unduly influenced by contemporary culture that uses these words in shallow ways that bear little resemblance to their meaning in the gospel?

Jesus' advice was for the disciples to be "wise as serpents and as innocent as doves" (Mt 10:16, NRSV). My goal is to help you to pray the Peace Prayer with "innocent wisdom," with both head and heart united in the spirit of the gospel so that you pray it as something of a promise freely given or a vow freely taken, and strive to live that vow in action every day.

May your use of this book and all you do to deepen your prayer open you to a greater share of the love and peace of Christ that we all seek.

James E. Adams

"Lord, make me . . ."

PRAYER MUST OPEN ME TO GOD'S WILL

"Not everyone who says to me, 'Lord, Lord,' will enter the kingdom of heaven, but only the one who does the will of my Father in heaven."

Matthew 7:21

In the very first word of the Peace Prayer, God is addressed as "Lord." "Lord" is much more than a formal address or title for God. Because of its long tradition in Christianity, "Lord" has become for many of us a rich prayer-word that elicits a profound sense of praise and respect. When I hear "Lord" in prayer or in scripture, I often feel as if I should be making a deep bow.

One dictionary definition for "Lord" is "one who has dominion over others; a master, chief, or ruler." When we address God as "Lord," we are acknowledging that we are not sovereign over ourselves, but are submissive to our Creator and gratefully obedient to our Redeemer. At least, we want to be. That is certainly a good start to any prayer. Indeed, could there be a better start?

However, as is the case with every step in our Christian journey, we need to heed the warnings we are given. The stark warning of Jesus given to us in Matthew reminds us how easily this wonderful start to our prayer can become little more than a hollow gesture. Unless our cry of "Lord, Lord," unless all our imploring of the Lord is followed by obedience to God's commands and desires, our prayer isn't likely to result in our transformation and growth in faith.

When we pray the Peace Prayer or any prayer, may we always strive to make our cry of "Lord, Lord" be a genuine act of worship that helps to open us to the sovereignty of God over all our thoughts and actions.

- Do I see myself as one who has the responsibility to discern and obey God's will not just occasionally but each day?
- Is my prayer centered on what I think I want or need or is it centered on learning and doing God's will?
- How much of God's plain and obvious will, such as charitable acts and living in solidarity with the poor, do I ignore day after day?

PRAYER IS AN ACT OF WORSHIP INSPIRED BY THE HOLY SPIRIT

Know that the LORD is God. It is he that made us, and we are his; we are his people, and the sheep of his pasture.

Psalm 100:3

What we ask for in the Peace Prayer or any prayer reveals what is valuable to us—or in some cases, what we think we should value. We trust that the Holy Spirit inspires us to ask for the right things in prayer. Yet we must always have the even more basic expectation that the Holy Spirit inspires us to pray, period.

What we pray for is secondary; *that* we pray is primary.

Prayer is homage, an old-fashioned word rarely used anymore. Homage has the Latin root "humus" (earth), the origin also of "humble." Would it even occur to us to reach out to God unless we realize that we are creatures and need to defer to our Creator? This, surely, is the psychological bedrock of prayer. Prayer is a profound act of worship that we freely give when we sense who we are in relation to our Creator. The need to pray is what we sense when we know ourselves and when we know God.

The basic impulse to pray is something we share with Judaism and Islam. But in our Christian faith we have an additional incentive. The Creator has revealed a lavish plan of redemption, so that now we approach God as our loving Savior as well.

- Do I pray and seek to honor God daily?
- Am I mindful daily that God is my Creator and the Creator of all reality?
- What kind of prayer do I pray regularly or what discipline do I follow daily or frequently to stay aware of God as the source of all that I am and have?

Praying even when I'm not ready to do so wholeheartedly

"Lord, I am not worthy to have you come under my roof. . . ."

Matthew 8:8

I am asking the Lord for a great spiritual gift in the Peace Prayer. I am asking to live a life of gospel holiness, deep faith, compelling hope, and self-giving love. I am asking for the chance to be and to act Godlike. I am asking for the opportunity to show that I'm a disciple of Jesus in deed as well as in name.

I am asking for the opportunity to take the great risk of discovering for myself whether Jesus indeed has the secret to reality, that in giving over this fragile, severely flawed, makeshift entity called me, I'll ultimately receive unimaginable happiness through the real and renewed Godlike me that blossoms fully in eternity.

Do we really *want* to pray such a prayer? Many of us are caught in the dilemma of the young Augustine: he was moved to ask God to make him chaste and holy—but not just yet! Perhaps it would be more realistic to lower our goals and ask to be faithful in, say, the Ten Commandments rather than aspiring to become a self-giving instrument of God's peace.

No, the reach of our prayers must exceed the grasp. There may be times when we don't feel like praying a prayer that seems to put us on the spot as this one does. Yet we realize that we are called anew each day to live the gospel. We realize also that our responses of faith ultimately are based on our will rather than on our feelings. We choose this, knowing full well that we may not be ready to choose it with our whole heart and soul.

Let us humbly accept that, in our frailty, our "Lord, Lord" isn't always as wholehearted as we'd like, and that, even on our best days, our weak wills may seem to be hedging.

- Is my commitment to prayer too dependent on my mood or my feelings?
- Do I avoid some prayers because they seem to demand too much of me?
- Am I selling God—and myself—short in my prayer?

Lord, I Believe—Abolish My Unbelief!

Ask in faith, never doubting, for the one who doubts is like a wave of the sea, driven and tossed by the wind; for the doubter, being doubled-minded and unstable in every way, must not expect to receive anything from the Lord.

James 1:6-8

Isn't it a little startling to our ears that this first request to God in the Peace Prayer is so blunt? "Make me . . ." No ifs, ands, or buts. Just "Lord, make this happen." "Do this." No hedging. No qualification.

Nowadays we tend to soften the wording of such requests. We might say something like, "Lord, please help me to become . . ." or, "Lord, if it is your will, grant me the grace to be. . . ." Somehow it sounds more polite to say it that way.

Yet there is something refreshing about such a plain, unvarnished request (demand, even!) of God. It resembles that most basic of biblical prayer forms, the psalm. When we pray, we don't need a lot of "whereas" clauses to try to remind God that he has the power to do what we are asking.

When we ask God for something, we are well-advised to do so in a way that shows we have no doubt that God wants to—and can—give us what we're asking for.

Lord, I believe you can make me an instrument of your peace and a faithful follower of the gospel. Help me to move beyond the doubts that may be preventing that from happening.

I PRAY FREELY AND FULLY WHEN
I REALIZE GOD IS IN CONTROL

"You are worthy, our Lord and God,
to receive glory and honor and power,
for you created all things,
and by your will they existed and were created."

Revelation 4:11

We eagerly call upon the Lord only when we appreciate fully that we are creatures—and that, ultimately, we are not in control.

We must frequently ask, "How much have I been influenced by the 'enlightened secularism' of this age, which tells me God is an irrelevant footnote to progressive human history and urges me to rely on myself for all I am, do, or have?"

"You're in control," the voice of secularism says, "and if any progress is to be made, it's up to you alone to do it." The demand this puts on us can be overwhelming. The weaker our faith in God as Creator and Sustainer of all, the more burdens we subconsciously put on ourselves.

That's why a fresh awareness of myself as a creature is so profoundly liberating. Imagine the deep sigh of relief when it dawns on me that I'm not the only—much less the most important—player on the stage of my life. I can relax once I begin to accept myself for what I truly am, a creature dependent on God to be filled and fulfilled. That is the truth about myself that can begin to set me free. That truth frees me to do more, not less, for myself.

If I am living this truth, then prayer becomes as natural as breathing. Prayer becomes something I'm drawn to.

- What self-images control my daily life?
- Do I see myself first and foremost in relation to God or do I, for all practical purposes, ignore God?
- Does my prayer life reveal a growing relationship with God or does it reveal a weak and failing one?

Beware turning worship and prayer into idolatry

I will . . . ascribe righteousness to my Maker.

Job 36:3

If praying originates as an act of worship to our Maker, is every act of praying good regardless of the sentiments in the person's heart? No, as the parable of the Pharisee and the tax collector in Luke 18:9-14 clearly shows.

Just because I recognize and acknowledge God in the act of praying doesn't mean I rightly understand the implications of who I am or who God is. "Bad faith," bad motives, can generate not only bad content for articulated prayer, but would seem to corrupt the very act of praying, even if the words are on some level true.

The Pharisee was "praying," and so presumably paying homage to God. Moreover, in his prayer of thanksgiving ("God, I *thank* you that I am not like other people . . ."), all his claims about himself apparently were true. The Pharisee was accurately reporting his good deeds and accomplishments; he *was* better than others. Yet his prayer was radically distorting the significance his religious deeds had on his relationship to God and to others.

The parable, remember, is about "some who trusted in themselves that they were righteous and regarded others with contempt." Our "righteousness," the grace to stand in relationship with God, does not originate with us. The Pharisee was mistaken in thinking that he could earn his right relationship with God even with intrinsically religious acts such as praying and tithing. His praying was not so much worship honoring God as it was idolatry, honoring himself and his own moral achievements.

- When I pray, who am I honoring, God or myself? My family? My church? My country?
- How often is my prayer thinly disguised self-congratulation?
- Does my prayer of thanksgiving help move me closer to gospel living, to knowing, loving, and serving God?

"Praying as if everything depended on me"

So it depends not on human will or exertion, but on God. . . .

Romans 9:16

You've probably heard the saying: "Pray as if everything depended on God, but work as if everything depended on you." I sometimes think that this is neither good theology nor good psychology.

To "work as if everything depended on you" would mean that prayer would soon disappear entirely. When I'm acting as if everything depends on me, I'm moving God out of the picture in a way that can't be restored by merely reciting prayers. Why would I bother to pray if I undertook all my work in a way that began by excluding my dependence on God?

Surely it's much more helpful to begin with the premise that God's role is to give and my role is to receive. Then I can easily invert this old saying on prayer: "Work as if everything depended on God, and pray as if everything depended on me." I will find it easier to work more calmly, with less anxiety and more detachment, if I realize that God ultimately brings my work to fruition. And I'm encouraged to pray more ardently when I realize that praying is one of my key roles as a dependent creature.

Loving God, help me to ground my prayer and all my spiritual efforts in a profound awareness of you as the giver of all good gifts in my life—including the desire to pray and spend time in your presence.

Franciscan Spiritual Center
6902 SE Lake Road Suite 300
Milwaukie, OR 97267-2148

BEWARE OF ASKING: WHAT CAN *I* DO FOR GOD?

"I am the vine, you are the branches. Those who abide in me and I in them bear much fruit, because apart from me you can do nothing."

John 15:5

In my generation, there clearly was a sense that it was better to storm heaven with good deeds than with prayer. It was part of a "can-do" attitude, perhaps best summarized by President John F. Kennedy's line urging, "Ask not what your country can do for you, but what you can do for your country." Many activist Christians, indeed, ask themselves "not what God can do for me, but what *I* can do for God." This attitude has a noble and unselfish side, but it can also reveal an arrogant approach in which the Creator-creature relationship is radically altered, even reversed.

When praying the Peace Prayer, we ask God to "make us" be and do great things for ourselves and others. Because we are asking for something so great, we need to be alert to an arrogance that may be slipping into our prayer and dulling a genuinely prayerful spirit. To pray the Peace Prayer in the right spirit, the humble spirit so clearly exemplified by St. Francis of Assisi, we must be in a realistically dependent position before God. How far are we slipping from the spirit of the "Our Father," in which we commit ourselves to God's agenda as spelled out in the gospel? If we discover that our prayer amounts to something like a press release announcing to God and the world all the good things we intend to do for God and others, we need to stop immediately and begin some serious soul-searching.

Of course, the point is not just that we manage to articulate a prayer that *sounds* humble, but rather that our prayer *is* humble because we know and enjoy our rightful place before God.

Loving Father, grant me the grace to listen to what you ask of me and to be receptive to the good things you intend to do for me. And, ultimately, through me.

"Lord, make me an instrument . . ."

An instrument in God's hand

*But the Lord said to him, "Go, for he is an instrument
whom I have chosen to bring my name before Gentiles
and kings and before the people of Israel."*

Acts 9:15

What we're asking in the first petition of the Peace
Prayer is enough to make us stop in our tracks. Of all
things to ask to become—an *instrument*! Who wants to
think of themselves nowadays as a *tool* to be used by
another (even if the Other is God and even if the cause is
noble)? If we were writing this prayer today, we'd probably
want to make more of an accommodation to self-
determination. Perhaps we'd change the word to
"channel" (which some do) to take some of the sting out
of "instrument" or to turn the whole concept into
something like "Lord, make me a full partner on your
peace team."

Yet we acknowledge in this petition that we normally
don't know how to be instruments, how best to use our
gifts and talents. We don't know in the many situations
we face what we should do and what God wants. We're
asking God to show us the divine will and to help us live
it.

Remember that instruments are, in essence, potentialities waiting to be evolved. Instruments are only as good as their designers, and cannot reach their potential except in the hands of skilled and devoted artisans. One of the highest compliments paid to exceptionally gifted musicians is that they "make their instruments come alive."

Could we do much better than to think of ourselves as potentialities designed by God the Creator awaiting the careful fine-tuning and virtuoso performance of the Holy Spirit?

Still, I suspect it isn't going to be easy for us to slide past "instrument." If we really want to make this prayer our own, we will probably need to meet the implications of "instrument" head-on. The first hurdle is imagining ourselves surrendering to God, becoming willing instruments of God's grace, the kind St. Francis became. That St. Paul became. That all the other great saints became. Just as the saints were invited, so are we invited to ask that God and the gospel become so dominant in our lives that we are nothing but tools in God's hand.

That "nothing but tools" does not make us inhuman, but rather fulfills our human destiny revealed by Christ.

• Am I willing to think of myself as God's instrument or do I strongly resist the notion?

- How many other less-than-Godly things, people, or institutions over the years have I, in effect, irresponsibly become a willing instrument for?
- What kind of instrument do I imagine myself to be?

THE MIGHTY ORCHESTRA OF DIVINE PEACE

*My heart is steadfast, O God, my heart is steadfast;
I will sing and make melody.*

Psalm 108:1

Rather than thinking of ourselves only as a tool in the context of the Peace Prayer, it might also be helpful for us to think of ourselves as a member of a large choir or as a musical instrument in a large orchestra. Then we would be asking something like this: "Lord, help me do my part by being the instrument I'm called to be in your orchestra that is making the beautiful music of your peace."

When we think of being an instrument alongside others in a mighty orchestra, we can tap into a rich layer of meaning and purpose that isn't obvious when we think only of being a tool doing an isolated task. Each of us is part of a whole and we each have our individual parts to play. We can't hear the whole of the music of peace that God is making out of our individual histories or of human history. Yet our faith assures us that it is happening, and that in eternity we will hear and appreciate God's peace as a beautiful symphony. In eternity, we will also hear and appreciate fully for the first time those few but rich notes we play in the cosmic symphony of God's peace.

Through faith, then, being called to be an "instrument" of God's peace becomes a reason for profound gratitude and celebration.

Thank you, loving God, for giving me a part to play in the divine peace you are bringing about. May I recognize my part, be grateful for it, and play it joyfully.

BECOMING THE INSTRUMENT GOD WANTS ME TO BE

But we have this treasure in clay jars, so that it may be made clear that this extraordinary power belongs to God and does not come from us.

2 Corinthians 4:7

We must examine our hearts to discern what kind of instruments we may be expecting ourselves to become. Am I asking to become the instrument *God* wants, but inwardly demanding to be only the instrument *I* want to be? Do I have a realistic view of my role in bringing God's peace to others? Am I expecting too much of myself? Or perhaps too little of myself?

May we pray the Peace Prayer in the spirit of humility of St. Francis. Let us not demand to be perfect instruments, to be better instruments than our brothers and sisters, or to be some kind of exotic instruments we aren't called to be. At the same time, let us have the courage to respond generously if we are being called to be extraordinary instruments, if we, indeed, are being called to respond to demands we'd prefer to ignore.

May we accept the limitations of the earthen vessels, the "clay jars" that we are, realizing always that the treasure we hold is a gift from God.

Lord, show me the kind of instrument of your peace you want me to be today—and help me to fulfill that role freely and fully.

"Lord, make me an instrument
of your peace . . ."

TO KNOW GOD, I NEED TO BE STILL

Be still, and know that I am God!

Psalm 46:10

The focus of the Peace Prayer seems to be primarily on doing wonderful things for, to, and with others. But interacting with others in such a self-giving way won't happen unless we are first nourished by God in deep, personal prayer. How can we foster peace in the hearts of others unless we ourselves are tapped into Christ's peace through prayer? And this means not just recitation of prayers, but time reserved for being alone in the presence of God in silence.

With the prevailing image of St. Francis as a kind of spiritual Johnny Appleseed going around preaching and doing good, it's easy to forget the vital role of personal prayer in St. Francis's life. But the practice of silent prayer is among the top principles of Franciscan spirituality. St. Francis urged his followers to nurture in their hearts a dwelling place for God. "Wherever we are, wherever we go, we bring our (monastic) cell with us," he said.

He set up many hermitages (usually caves) within a day's walk of where he was preaching or begging—so that he and his brothers were never very far from places of silent prayer. He often took several friars with him to a hermitage. As he began speaking out loud to himself, the brothers were to keep walking backward till they could hear him no more. At that distance, they kept watch so that no one disturbed St. Francis during his long hours of silent prayer.

- Have I set aside time daily for silent prayer?
- Do I need to take a day off periodically for silence and solitude?
- Do I need to schedule at least one weekend a year for a retreat?

DON'T GIVE THIS KIND OF PRAYER A SECOND THOUGHT!

For my thoughts are not your thoughts, nor are your ways my ways, says the LORD.

Isaiah 55:8

The value of silent, contemplative prayer that became second-nature to St. Francis and many other saints through the centuries is more important today than ever. It's called wordless prayer of the heart, or more commonly "centering" prayer.

The crucial first step of this prayer is detaching ourselves from what is the most familiar and the most intimate to us—and the most demanding—our thoughts. What is the one process that runs on and on virtually beyond our control every single waking moment? That sets the agenda for virtually everything we do? Our thoughts! In centering prayer, we strive to let go of our words, thoughts, and emotions without paying them any special heed.

We are thinking and emotive beings, so it would be fruitless to try to stop all our thoughts. That would be as unnatural—and impossible—as trying to stop our breathing. During the recommended twenty to thirty minutes of centering prayer at least once daily, we stop paying attention to our thoughts and emotions; insofar as possible, we let them just float by without judging or evaluating them or investing anything in them. We just let them pass through, almost as if we were a disinterested or absent third party.

What good does such an exercise do? When our hearts aren't centered on our ego-generated words, thoughts, and emotions, we are better primed to receive God's grace, to rest in the reality of the divine now. We're allowing ourselves to dwell in the healing and transforming presence of the God of whom all our images (thoughts included) are inadequate anyway, if not false and idolatrous. Centering prayer involves the spiritual discipline of reducing the hold our thought-producing egos have over the totality of our lives, and of making an opening that allows greater influence of the Holy Spirit who dwells within us already.

- Do I take time to examine how the uninterrupted and free flow of words, thoughts, and emotions sets the agenda for my life and may well control my life in unhealthy ways?
- Do I have any exercises to discipline my unchecked thought process? To reduce its dominating hold on my life?

In "centering prayer"
we give a little but get a lot

"Give, and it will be given to you. A good measure, pressed down, shaken together, running over, will be put into your lap; for the measure you give will be the measure you get back."

Luke 6:38

Many who ignore or reject the gospel, it has been observed, do so because what it promises is just too good to believe. God just can't be offering so much to us for so little from us. When push comes to shove, God can't really be the pushover "Prodigal Father" depicted in the gospels.

Something close to that can be said about "centering" prayer, the discipline of simply sitting comfortably, eyes closed with a minimum of incoming stimuli, for twenty-five minutes at least once a day (preferably, twice) with the intention of resting in God's presence. Give God these precious few minutes each day and God will begin filling you with the divine Self. Some who might otherwise be attracted to such prayer find the promise of its benefits just too good to believe.

One gives to God two simple things anyone is capable of giving—time and intention. What is twenty-five minutes of our time and intention? Not much. But when you give the little you have each day, that's all God needs. Through faith we come to realize that our "little" seems to be what brings out God's "much," that the divine economy isn't based on the copper standard of the limited value of the human giver and of what's given, but on the gold standard of the infinite value of the One who receives what is offered, thereby enhancing it a hundredfold.

In our relationship with God we can be grateful that "the measure you give will be the measure you get back" isn't literally true. What we get back is boundless because it is measured by the generosity of the divine receiver and not by the limits of the human giver.

- Do I become discouraged when my prayer seems so poor?
- When I can't give much, do I abandon trying to give even a little?
- Am I trying to do much with little faith and love rather than trying to do a little with much faith and love?

We don't seek peace—we seek God

"Teacher, which commandment in the law is the greatest?" He said to him, "'You shall love the Lord your God, with all your heart, and with all your soul, and with all your mind.' This is the greatest and first commandment."

Matthew 22:36-38

In our journey to and with Christ, we are not asking for peace for its own sake. We cannot make peace-seeking or even peace-making the first goal of our spiritual journey as Christians. We don't first seek peace, and in that peace somehow find God. We first and always seek God—and then we learn to be content with whatever portion of divine peace God deems to give us in this world. Indeed, the peace of Christ may not seem very peaceful at all by any of our normal worldly standards.

Ironically, peace isn't the most important thing in the Peace Prayer. God and our relationship to God is the crucial, if unspoken, business of the Peace Prayer. Peace doesn't lead us to God; peace follows from a right relationship to God. Peace is among the things given to us when we "strive first for the kingdom of God" (Mt 6:33).

- How often does a desire for "peace" rather than the desire to know and love God motivate me?
- For whom or what am I "striving first" in my life?

THE PEACE OF CHRIST IS AT
THE HEART OF THE GOSPEL

"Peace I leave with you; my peace I give to you."

John 14:27

"Peace" is a key word in Christian revelation, appearing more than one hundred times in scripture. Peace, indeed, is central to the gospel. Our Father is called a God of peace (1 Cor 14:33) who sends his Son Jesus, who is "our peace" (Eph 2:14). Peace is first and last in the gospel accounts. At Jesus' birth the angelic chorus sings: "Glory to God in the highest heaven, and on earth peace among those whom he favors" (Lk 2:14). In his parting speech to the disciples, Jesus says, "Peace I leave with you; my peace I give to you" (Jn 14:27). In John's gospel and Paul's epistles, "peace" becomes virtually synonymous with redemption, salvation, eternal life—or is linked directly with them.

Although the Peace Prayer is ecumenical and broad-reaching, it cannot be reduced to a humanistic prayer with no link to the gospel. We pray this prayer as faithfully as we can only when we link it to the profound meaning of "peace" from our Christian tradition.

- Do I appreciate the biblical meaning of peace as the redemption brought by Jesus?

- Do I think of peace as something manufactured here below rather than as given from above?
- Do I see peace as a gift, like faith, that must be sought and nurtured daily?

GIVING RESPECT TO
EVERYONE AND EVERYTHING

O LORD, how manifold are your works!
In wisdom you have made them all;
the earth is full of your creatures.

Psalm 104:24

Among the stories about St. Francis that may strike us today as quaint are accounts of the profound reverence he showed toward every person, every creature, every thing. He went to great lengths to avoid embarrassing a brother. Any abuse of animals saddened him deeply. He is said often to have stopped to pick up worms trying to wiggle across roads and carefully put them in the safety of weeds alongside the road.

The deep reverence and respect that St. Francis held for all reality flowed from the generous heart of a mystic. When he encountered other beings, his initial reaction was not one of fear, arrogance, or greed. His response was not based on how other people, animals, or things might be helpful or harmful to him. Rather, his initial reaction seemed to be: here's a fellow creature who has as much right to exist and to flourish as I do.

Where there is such profound reverence and respect for all creatures, there would naturally follow a great desire for peace.

- How respectful am I of other people? Of other creatures? Of material things?
- Can I appreciate God's creatures for what they are rather than only for what they can do for me?

Can the peace of Christ be "enforced"?

"When they bring you to trial and hand you over, do not worry beforehand about what you are to say; but say whatever is given you at that time, for it is not you who speak, but the Holy Spirit."

Mark 13:11

Some years ago the U.S. military had a missile that was nicknamed "The Peacemaker," a name first used for a favorite handgun of "peace officers" in the Wild West. So naming lethal instruments may seem an innocent extension of "keeping the peace," that is, maintaining public order by force or threat of force. Yet isn't there something odd or even perverse about linking weapons that maim and kill with "peace," especially the peace of Christ that we are talking about in this prayer?

If we pray in the spirit of St. Francis, we cannot ask for the power to enforce something—anything—on others. Indeed, we are asking for no power, only the spiritual power that flows out of the powerlessness of love. We are asking for the grace to give ourselves in love as Jesus gave himself in love.

St. Francis renounced all external power, and was apparently leery even of ecclesiastical power. Incoming friars who were ordained were allowed to join, but those who weren't apparently were not to be ordained. It is disputed whether the founder ever gave his blessing for the friars to study theology. Whatever the details of this dispute, one thing seems clear: St. Francis wanted his followers to be "unarmed" in their peacemaking mission, to give up even the psychological advantage over others that they might have by virtue of clerical authority or theological knowledge and training that might have made them haughty and domineering.

Now that's a radical commitment to the gospel—refusing to bear or use even spiritual arms, but depending instead only on the inspiration of the Holy Spirit!

- What role does physical, psychological, or moral force—or the threat of such force—play in my relationship with others?
- If I am in a leadership position in a family or a community, is my use of force necessary and appropriate?
- Is my use of force haughty and domineering?

THE PEACE OF CHRIST DOESN'T MEAN
THE END OF CONFLICTS

*"Peace I leave with you; my peace I give to you. I do
not give to you as the world gives."*

John 14:27

We can be sure the "peace" of this Franciscan-
inspired prayer isn't the securing of a convenient
compromise. The object of this peace isn't satisfaction of
our natural human desire to be at rest, to be free from any
and all conflict, to take the course of least resistance, to be
content, to have no cares. After his conversion, St. Francis
probably didn't enjoy a single day of such peace. There
were many conflicts and disputes that caused him
heartaches as the rules for the fledgling order of "Little
Brothers" were being hammered out.

How easy it is to delude ourselves into thinking that
we are seeking to further the peace of Christ in our world
when, in fact, we may well just be seeking to escape the
daily conflicts of a genuine Christian discipleship.

We must beware of letting the Peace Prayer become
for even an instant a wistful, sentimentalized plea for
general amity. What we are asking to foster is the peace of
Christ. The peace of Christ inevitably brings tension with

the peace of this world, and it is a tension we can expect to last until the Second Coming.

- Say the word "peace" to yourself several times. What does the word bring to mind?
- Now say the words "peace of Christ" to yourself several times. What does that bring to mind?

"PEACE" MAY BRING
CONFLICT AND ALIENATION

"I have not come to bring peace, but a sword."

Matthew 10:34

We should never confuse Franciscan-inspired peacemaking with the political skill of getting along with anybody and everybody. Peacemaking for St. Francis is work! It began with a purifying of his own heart so that he could know and live the gospel of divine forgiveness and love, even if that put him sharply at odds with others, including his own family.

Soon after St. Francis answered the call to radical gospel holiness, there was a showdown in the town square of Assisi. Rather than agreeing to rejoin his family and return to the values of the merchant middle class his father championed, St. Francis stripped off all his clothes and declared that he would henceforth call "father" only his heavenly Father. This outraged his father. As far as is known, St. Francis and his father never reconciled, even though near his death St. Francis was said to have regrets that he hadn't done so.

This is a stark reminder to all who pray the Peace Prayer that the peace of Christ is fully realized only in eternity, and that the peace of Christ we seek to foster in this life may not always bring a peaceful coexistence with others.

- In what situations in my life do I let the fear of conflict, confrontation, or alienation prevent me from being the instrument of peace I know God is calling me to be?
- What do I need to do to learn how better to live in God's peace even amid conflicts in my family and at work?

PEACE BREAKS OUT ONLY
WHEN JUSTICE IS SERVED

Love and truth will meet;
justice and peace will kiss.

Psalm 85:11 (NAB)

Would it detract from the spirit of the Peace Prayer if "justice" were used instead of "peace"? No—and injecting "justice" might help restore some of the depth the word "peace" has lost for many people.

The foundation for peace is the realization of the justice of God, when creatures begin to give God and others their due. Peace for Christian disciples comes when justice is being done, namely when they are loving God with their whole hearts, minds, and souls, and when they are loving others in and for the love of Christ. This is Christ's "law" of love. It is what we *owe* God and *owe* others, and until we serve justice by paying those "debts," there is no peace.

When we talk of helping to bring others "peace," we may tend to think we are bringing something extra for which they aren't really entitled. But when we bring divine "justice" into the picture, we are praying for the grace to do what we were created to do. We are asking for help to give God and others their due—a full measure of our love and service.

> *Lord, help me to see that doing my part to bring justice and peace to others isn't just an optional exercise of religious piety but is my fundamental calling as a Christian.*

ACCEPTING INJUSTICE IS A PHONY PEACE

Woe to those who call evil good, and good evil, who change darkness into light, and light into
darkness.

Isaiah 5:20 (NAB)

Beware of praying in effect: "Lord, let me help others find 'spiritual' peace, but I don't want to know anything about or get involved in social movements or political causes that might address specific injustices against others." Indeed, we'd be making a mockery of this prayer if we somehow sought to help others find only a false "peace" that came from accepting the injustices perpetrated against them.

In the Peace Prayer, we are asking to be open to see and respond to injustices suffered by individuals around us, in our families, at work, or in our church groups and communities. We must beware of thinking in abstractions, of working up a rich moral lather about dramatic injustices halfway around the world while ignoring less publicized but no less real injustices against individuals much closer to home, perhaps even within our own homes.

- Do I try to be aware of injustices in my family, community, and the world?

- Do I support those who suffer injustices?
- Do I encourage others to resist injustices perpetrated against them?
- Do I resist injustices done to me?

"Where there is hatred,
let me sow love . . ."

How pervasive human hatred is!

*For we ourselves were once foolish . . . passing our days
in malice and envy, despicable, hating one another.*

Titus 3:3

Does the phrase "where there is hatred" seem to have a naive ring, as if the author might be assuming hatred is rare? Sadly, we know that hatred isn't rare. It is common as dirt. When we pray this prayer, we should have a realistic view of the pervasiveness of hatred. We can be sure that St. Francis, even though an idealist, knew well the potential for hate in the human heart.

The Book of Wisdom says Satan was envious of the happiness of humans, hated us, and so delivered the world over to death and hatred (Wis 2:24). Hatred reared up in the first generations of humans, as Cain was so consumed by it that he killed his brother Abel. The sad fact is that hate seems to be universal and inevitable—apart from the redemption of Christ. Left to our unredeemed selves, we easily fall prey to hate, perhaps not the hate that ends in murder but certainly the hate that divides us from others.

How great is the need for this prayer! There is a lot of love to sow because there is a lot of hate. Is there any devotion more needful and more worthwhile than to pray this prayer every day with conviction and to commit ourselves to putting it into practice?

- Do I have a view of the human condition based on Christian realism?
- In what ways is my understanding of human nature too romantic and superficial?
- Am I aware of any hatred directed toward me?
- Do I frequently give in to feelings of hatred toward others?

Do I realize *I* need to be saved from hate?

"How can you say to your neighbor, 'Let me take the speck out of your eye,' while the log is in your own eye?"

Matthew 7:4

When you hear the phrase "where there is hatred, let me sow love," do you immediately think of hatred "out there"? I do. The habit of seeing the splinter in others' eyes while being oblivious to the log in our own comes easily. Could it be that the very first place with its share of hate that needs love is your very own heart? Yes, count on it. We must be aware of the hatred and ill will that we may be harboring against others, acknowledge it, and seek to neutralize it by loving aspirations and actions.

As with all the petitions of the Peace Prayer, I cannot pray this petition as if I am the physician and others are my patients, as if I am the giver while others are receivers, as if I'm full and others are empty.

I can only pray it as one who knows through the gift of faith how loveless and hateful I am, how profoundly in need of redemption I stand, and yet to what heights of selfless holiness I am called by God's grace.

I can dare to ask to sow love amid hatred only because I know that the love of Christ is being sown daily amid the hatred of my own divided heart.

Lord, help me to learn from you the gentleness and humility of heart I need to live the Peace Prayer.

SOW FORGIVING LOVE FIRST IN MY OWN HEART

The heart is devious above all else; it is perverse—who can understand it? I the Lord test the mind and search the heart. . . .

Jeremiah 17:9-10

When we pray the Peace Prayer, we must be aware of the hatred and ill will that we may be half-consciously harboring against ourselves. That might be the last thing many of us would think of. But think again. We know the dangers of excessive self-love. We have been duly warned about self-righteousness and the ease with which we deceive ourselves, turning our evil into good by our clever rationalizations. But when our religious response tends to be too intellectualized, we can become relentlessly critical and very demanding of ourselves without even noticing it. At the very least, many of us today maintain a deep mistrust of our ability to evaluate our own spiritual health.

Being aware of—and accepting—our moral and spiritual limitations is the beginning of gospel wisdom and holiness. However, we must examine ourselves to make sure that our self-criticism hasn't degenerated into self-denigration or even self-loathing.

Lord, help me to see that the place that most needs the sowing of your forgiving love is my own heart.

"Where there is hatred, let me sow love; where there is injury, pardon . . . doubt, faith . . . despair, hope . . . darkness, light . . . sadness, joy . . ."

DARE I ASPIRE TO GOALS SHORT OF MY CALLING?

"Very truly, I tell you, the one who believes in me will also do the works that I do and, in fact, will do greater works than these. . . ."

John 14:12

We cannot pray the Peace Prayer eagerly or live it fully until we begin to see ourselves as disciples called to live the life Jesus himself lived. Yes, we are challenged to think of ourselves as brothers and sisters of Jesus called to the same heights of self-giving love as Jesus. Bringing love for hatred, pardon for injury, faith for doubt, hope for despair, light for darkness, and joy for sadness was what Jesus did. Resisting evil with good was what Jesus did during his sojourn on earth.

This pattern of resisting evil with good followed from Jesus' relationship with the Father. Easy for him to do, we might object, because *he* was the Son of God. But Jesus revealed that *we* also are sons and daughters of God, and he promised that we can do even greater things than he because of *our* relationship to the Father and the gifts of the Holy Spirit.

Soren Kierkegaard wrote: "Christ comes to the world as the example, constantly enjoining: Imitate me. We humans prefer to adore him instead."

We are called not just to believe *in* Jesus in the sense that we trust he has saved us, and given us scripture, the sacraments, and the church to help us get to heaven. We are also called to believe *as* Jesus believed—to respond to life as Jesus responded.

- Do I often ignore or play down my calling to believe and to live as Jesus did?
- Do I see as my basic Christian calling to strive to respond to others the way Jesus responded to them?
- Do I use worship of God as an excuse to avoid the call to become Godlike myself, to respond in a Godlike way to others?

COMPASSION IS CALLED FOR
EVERYWHERE AND ALWAYS

As God's chosen ones, holy and beloved, clothe yourselves with compassion, kindness, humility, meekness, and patience. Bear with one another, and . . . forgive each other.

Colossians 3:12-13

The Peace Prayer surely sprung from the heart of a compassionate person who knew well the bitter realities of the sin-crippled human life everyone experiences. Not St. Francis, as we know, but someone who had Franciscan sensitivities. This prayer is about the troubles and tragedies of daily life that no individual, no family, no community ever escapes entirely. It is a prayer suited above all for the daily grind in the home and in the workplace.

Where is there injury, and doubt, and hatred, and despair, and darkness, and sadness? Everywhere humans live, work, and play!

If we want to see the compelling need to pray this prayer, all we have to do is open our eyes and look around at ourselves and others. Not a day—probably not even an hour—goes by when we aren't presented with opportunities to help turn hatred into love, injury into pardon, doubt into faith, despair into hope, darkness into light, sadness into joy. Opportunities are right here, right now.

- Have I recently tried to turn hatred into love, injury into pardon?
- Do I frequently shut my mind and heart to the pain and suffering around me?
- Do I deny my own pain and suffering?
- Do I tend to be judgmental in my reactions to others, assuming they get what they deserve in life?

IF I'M SELF-ABSORBED, I WON'T
PRAY THE PEACE PRAYER

*Bear one another's burdens, and in this way you will
fulfill the law of Christ.*

Galatians 6:2

With so much injury, doubt, despair, darkness, and
sadness in and around us, why isn't the Peace Prayer more
earnestly prayed and practiced? The most obvious reason
perhaps is selfishness. Or more likely, self-absorption. By
the time we've dealt with our own pain, how can we have
anything left to give others? By the time we've come to
terms with our own injury, doubt, despair, darkness, and
sadness, who has the energy left to think about others?
Somehow, this seems to limit us even when we know our
own troubles may be trifling by comparison.

Many of us have become adept at ignoring the pain of
others, no doubt as a simple survival tactic. We tell
ourselves we can't be expected to "bear one another's
burdens," not with so many so heavily burdened. Yet we
cannot continually close our hearts to the needs of others
and still consider ourselves faithful Christians. We are
called to pray and to live the Peace Prayer because we are
members of the Body of Christ.

- Do I believe that Christians are called to bear each other's burdens?
- Am I actively trying at this time to bear at least one other person's burdens?
- Do I recognize the burdens I'm carrying?
- Am I bearing my own burdens patiently and seeking help from others when my burdens become too tiresome?

Peace prayer ideals are easy for us to identify with

He it is who gave himself for us that he might redeem us from all iniquity and purify for himself a people of his own who are zealous for good deeds.

Titus 2:14

Identifying with the aspirations of the Peace Prayer would seem to be easy. The noble sentiments of peace-producing love for and service to others have a strong natural appeal. By our very nature, who of us prefers to be hateful to others rather than loving? Who of us prefers to tolerate and promote hatred when confronted by a choice between it and love? We just aren't made that way. Who of us wouldn't want to bring hope rather than despair, light rather than darkness, joy rather than sadness?

Many of us might try to live so that rarely do we have to help others meet their physical and spiritual needs. Many of us may try to live as much of our lives as we can without being forced to clarify the ethical demands on us of responding to specific instances of hatred, injury, doubt, despair, darkness, and sadness. But faced with the choice, is there any doubt what we'd choose? We'll choose love over hatred every time. What we might actually do in real-life situations to bring love, pardon, faith, hope, light, and joy could sour and bring hatred, injury, doubt, despair, darkness, and sadness instead. But that's not what we *intended*, not what we wanted.

Who would actually pray for or seek the strength to sow hatred rather than love? We would probably say such a one was so sick, demonic, or hopelessly victimized by circumstances beyond their control as to have been rendered temporarily inhuman (not just *unChristian*). St. Thomas Aquinas defined us as beings motivated ultimately by what we perceive as the good, however misguided our perception might be.

Praying the Peace Prayer provides an opportunity for us to reaffirm the choice to go in the direction our hearts lean—namely toward love, pardon, faith, hope, light, and joy rather than toward hatred, injury, doubt, despair, darkness, and sadness.

However, precisely because these sentiments are frequently so easy for us to affirm in prayer, we have to be especially alert to what might be called an "inoculation effect." We may so genuinely profess in prayer our earnest and wholehearted devotion to bringing love, pardon, faith, hope, light, and joy that it begins to feel almost as if we've already done it in the real world.

- Do the warm feelings I get during public and private prayer lead me to lift the burdens of others?

- Or does my prayer become a substitute for actually helping others?
- Does my prayer lead me toward gospel holiness or toward self-centeredness?

LIVING THE PEACE PRAYER ONE DAY AT A TIME

"My grace is sufficient for you, for power is made perfect in weakness."

2 Corinthians 12:9

To pray the Peace Prayer with full devotion is to commit ourselves daily to bringing love amid hatred, pardon amid injury, faith amid doubt, hope amid despair, light amid darkness, and joy amid sadness. Isn't that too much to ask of ourselves each day? There may be many times when we feel we should declare, "Oh, no. Not me. Not today."

Yes, the Peace Prayer is too much for us—but not for the Holy Spirit praying in us. As with all Christian prayer and practice, we look to God's strength while acknowledging our own weakness.

Praying and striving to live the Peace Prayer *daily* is precisely what we must do as creatures of habit to keep open access to God's grace. If we say we're closing the door of our heart for a while, we immediately put ourselves on a slippery slope. Daily habits have a cumulative effect and help reinforce our good intentions and acts. We take unnecessary risks when we suspend our daily devotional and religious commitments.

We must remain open to responding to *all* that might be demanded of us by God each and every day. Often we panic because we are looking beyond the day. In Matthew 6:34, Jesus says, "Sufficient for a day is its own evil." We might aptly paraphrase that by saying, "Sufficient for a day is the grace needed to do that day's good."

- Do I re-commit myself each day to live a life of gospel holiness and self-giving love?
- How often do I excuse myself from responding to Jesus' call to love others?

WE CAN MAKE A DIFFERENCE IN
THE LIVES OF OTHERS

Where sin increased, grace abounded all the more. . . .

Romans 5:20

Whenever anyone prays and aspires to the goals of the Peace Prayer, that in itself is a sign of grace and hope that should increase our confidence.

In the face of so much injury, doubt, despair, darkness, and sadness in our world, how easy it would be to say: "What's the use? We can't do anything against such odds. Better just to curse the darkness than waste our time trying to light little candles one at a time. We don't even know if those who are hurting want our help or will appreciate what we might be able to give. Let's just mind our own business and not get involved with others."

Instead, with the gifts of faith and the fortitude of the Holy Spirit, we realize that what we do for others who are injured, despairing, and sad matters—even though we may not know how much until years later. We can make a difference. We are not totally isolated from others. We can break through to them. It's worth the effort to try to make a connection with others who seem isolated by their pain.

Lord, help me to set a good example for others in my family and my community or parish by persisting daily in my effort to pray and to live the Peace Prayer.

PRAY FOR YOURSELF WHEN
YOUR NEED IS GREAT

"You shall love your neighbor as yourself."

Matthew 22:39

This is anything but a prayer exclusively about me or about my relationship to God in isolation from others. Christianity is not simply a matter of self-enrichment, but of caring concern for others. The Peace Prayer, above all others, looks outward to God and others rather than inwardly to the status of the pray-er. It's a prayer about giving to others, not a prayer about receiving for myself.

But can I be self-giving if I have no self to give? Or a self that is so badly wounded as to be paralyzed? How can I really love others if I don't love myself? What if my own personal spiritual relationship with God is anemic and stands in dire need of nourishment? Then, I might well begin praying the Peace Prayer as if I myself rather than others were most in need of love, pardon, faith, hope, light, and joy.

In that case, I would be praying for and committing myself to the work of my own healing as well as the healing of others.

O Loving God, I know I need your help to become the disciple I am called to be. Let the healing I most need in my life begin today.

LEARNING TO LIVE AMID THE FORCES OF EVIL

"Your heavenly Father . . . makes his sun rise on the bad and the good, and causes rain to fall on the just and the unjust."

Matthew 5:45 (NAB)

Most of us recognize isolated cases of hatred, injury, doubt, despair, darkness, and sadness that are so harmful that no rest can be taken until something is done to reduce the ill effects. Yet the move-heaven-and-earth urgency rightly felt in such cases should not be turned into an all-out, lifelong war on anything and everything that seems "evil."

Is that what we seek in the Peace Prayer? Are we asking for—and expecting to live to see—the complete eradication of hatred, injury, doubt, despair, darkness, and sadness in this world? No—and we can't if the prayer is to remain Christian at heart. To pray with such a goal and to live with the expectation that such a goal is possible, we would be inspired more by a romantic utopianism than by the gospel. The Christian worldview is not dualistic, where reality is to be judged as either unequivocally evil or good. The Christian worldview is bipolar, where reality is seen as a yet-unresolved (and unresolvable, except by God) mix of good and evil.

Recall the image Jesus uses in Matthew 13 about the kingdom of heaven being like a dragnet that holds an odd and scary assortment of all kinds of creatures. The implication is that as long as time endures, we are to live with this reality—only beyond time will angels sort good from evil. Recall also the parable of Jesus in Matthew 13 about the weeds and the wheat. The servants ask the householder if they should go into the wheat fields and try to pluck out the weeds. The answer is a startling one that overzealous Christians down through the ages often seem to forget. "No, for in gathering the weeds you would uproot the wheat along with them. Let both of them grow together until the harvest."

Lord, help me to strive for gospel holiness and to be an instrument of your peace without getting caught up in unrealistic and utopian goals.

THE PEACE PRAYER CALLS FOR
A ONE-ON-ONE MINISTRY

*Little children, let us love, not in word or speech, but
in truth and action.*

1 John 3:18

Sowing love, pardon, faith, hope, light, and joy where
there is hatred, injury, doubt, despair, darkness, and
sadness is not something we do *to* or *for* others, but rather
with them. We live the Peace Prayer fully when we join
those in need and do what we can to help them gain or
recover these spiritual goods in their lives.

There is no quick and easy way to be an instrument
of Christ's peace. The Peace Prayer is a call to a one-on-
one ministry. It implies a commitment if not to befriend
another, at least to enter into a relationship of trust with
another, to make ourselves available to another for more
than a few moments or a few hours. Such an ongoing
relationship takes time.

Almsgiving and many other isolated acts of concern
for others are fully in the spirit of the Peace Prayer. We
don't belittle those, however, if we note that this "Simple
Prayer" inspired by St. Francis calls for a much more
personal touch.

Lord, give me the discernment to see around me those who need my personal attention and care—and the courage to give it.

PEACE PRAYER ISN'T THE GRAND
PRAYER OF CO-DEPENDENCY!

"If anyone will not welcome you or listen to your words, shake off the dust from your feet as you leave that house or town."

Matthew 10:14

We're asking for the grace to *sow* love, pardon, faith, hope, light, and joy in the lives of others. We are not asking for the power to bestow it outright on others (presuming that were possible).

We are not asking for the power to do something for others or to try to do it in their stead. Rather, we are asking to be an instrument, a catalyst, a spark, helping others to gain or restore the love, pardon, faith, hope, light, and joy they may lack in their lives.

We realize nowadays more than ever before that individuals ultimately are responsible for themselves; they must personally exercise their freedoms if they are to be healed of addictions, disorders, failings, and sin.

Although we might be tempted to make it so, the Peace Prayer isn't the grand prayer of co-dependency. We can't make peace for others, we can't give them faith or hope, or take away their doubt or despair or sadness.

Ultimately, they must do that themselves—with God's grace and with our help.

Recall that the Prodigal Son reached rock bottom before he "came to his senses" and decided of his own accord to return to the father's house. Only then could the son benefit from the merciful bounty of the father.

• Do I frequently try to do things *for* others instead of *with* them?

AM I HELPING OTHERS GET OUT OF THEIR RUTS?

*And let us consider how to provoke one another to love
and good deeds, not neglecting to meet together, as is
the habit of some, but encouraging one another. . . .*

Hebrews 10:24-25

When we are living the Peace Prayer, we are helping
others free themselves from the hatred, injury, doubt,
despair, darkness, or sadness that binds them. We do not
know how long it might take in individual situations for
people to become free of what binds them. It might be
only hours or it might be weeks, months, or even years. If
we are persistent in our efforts to live the Peace Prayer, we
cannot be too hasty in trying to decide how much
progress is being made with others whom we are trying to
help by our listening and sharing.

Still, some movement, however modest, must occur
sooner or later. If we aren't interacting with others with
"tough love," our relationship with them may actually be
encouraging them to wallow in their hatred, injury, doubt,
despair, darkness, or sadness rather than challenging
them to move on. We aren't doing them a service if our
relationship with them is only helping them dig deeper the
rut they're in.

- In which of my relationships am I too passive?
- Are there some people in my life I need to challenge more directly and frequently?
- Do I, too, need to be challenged more directly by others?

Taking offense and giving offense

Let us therefore no longer pass judgment on one another, but resolve instead never to put a stumbling block or hindrance in the way of another.

Romans 14:13

Sometimes it seems that the world is made up of two kinds of people—those who give offense and those who take offense. In our Western culture, those who take offense seem to outnumber by far those who intentionally give offense. Most words weren't designed to offend others. But look at the hassles nowadays over some traditional personal, family, and gender wording that many people may use innocently enough, but which many others consider offensive or degrading.

Can't we just say: "To heck with it. If people take offense when I never intended any, that's their problem." But stop and think. If someone is sensitive to something, don't we have to assume the source is real? When my dentist is poking around and hits a sore spot in my gums, he takes note and doesn't try to convince me that the spot isn't sore! And although we both know the dentist didn't *intend* to, the poking hurt me, nonetheless.

No doubt, many injuries weren't intended. Does that mean we try to convince injured people that they aren't really hurting and that no pardon is needed in that situation? No, we have to assume there's an injury there that we need to do our part to heal.

- Do I frequently belittle or mock or play down the hurts of others?

A PLACE FOR DARKNESS IN OUR SPIRITUAL LIVES

*When it was noon, darkness came over the whole land
until three in the afternoon.*

Mark 15:33

When the darkness caused by sin or ignorance has us
or others we love imprisoned, we resist it and instinctively
want to shine as much light on it as quickly as possible.
Before we advance too quickly and heedlessly on any and
all darkness, however, we should reflect on the concept in
scripture and in Catholic spiritual traditions to assess
when some forms of darkness may be beneficial and need
to be befriended.

"Darkness" in scripture is frequently used poetically
in contrast to light. In other cases, darkness is a sign of
God's presence or the beginning of God's creative or
redemptive acts. Exodus 20:21 says Moses "drew near to
the thick darkness where God was." Darkness in such
cases signals that a saving event is about to happen. The
three-hour darkness at Jesus' death indicates a redemptive
event of cosmic significance, the start of a new creation as
it were, recalling the darkness over the earth in the
creation story in Genesis.

Consider the darkness of the tomb in which Jesus was
buried. That is a rich image of the hiddenness of grace,

reminding us that much of the mysterious working of redemption takes place in darkness beyond the reach of—or the need for—any light. Jesus in the tomb is not unlike that seed of which he spoke—the seed, having died, now has begun its growth in darkness. Only faith can penetrate such darkness and help us to see the workings of grace in our lives or the lives of others.

There are many echoes in Catholic prayer and spirituality of the "apophatic" tradition, the best known if often misunderstood phrase of which is "the dark night of the soul." Appreciation of darkness is a key element in this tradition, wherein darkness paradoxically signifies not the absence but the presence of God.

When such darkness is encountered by ourselves or others, rather than panic and fly blindly like moths toward the nearest bright light, we should pause and try to discern if it is signaling some profound spiritual opportunity or some call to conversion or growth.

- Do I insist that my religion provide clarity in everything?
- Do I demand clear answers to spiritual issues?
- Am I capable of sitting prayerfully and patiently in my own darkness? With others in their darkness? Perhaps even with my parish or church in its darkness?

REFLECTING THE LIGHT OF CHRIST

"For where two or three are gathered in my name, I am there among them."

Matthew 18:20

When we think of sowing light where there is darkness, we should neither underestimate nor overestimate our abilities. It's easy enough to assume we have little or no light to help others in their darkness. But all of us have more to offer than we realize. Have you had friends or family tell you years afterward how much they appreciated the advice or support or comfort you offered in a crisis or disruptive situation? Or have you been told you helped in a way you never dreamed? All of us have some light to share that can help others in some, if not all, the circumstances they find themselves caught in.

However, the light we may be able to shed for others shouldn't lead us to assume it's only *our* light or that we alone are its source. If we are acting out of love of God and neighbor, we can be bold enough to assume that we are reflecting the light of Christ. If we've helped others, it's more likely to be explained by Jesus' promise to be with his followers when they gather in his name than by any light we've generated on our own.

- Do I assume I have no light to offer others who are struggling with their darkness?
- What special gift or sensitivity could I bring to others in their times of darkness?

SOME SADNESS IS NORMAL AND INEVITABLE

For misery does not come from the earth, nor does trouble sprout from the ground; but human beings are born to trouble just as sparks fly upward.

Job 5:6-7

There are two kinds of responses to sadness in the gospels. One is the sadness-unto-despair that comes from realizing you have done evil or failed to do good—you lose all hope and desire of getting another chance to change or make amends. This was the response of Judas, and, in a milder form, of the rich young ruler who declined to sell his possessions and follow Jesus because he realized he was too attached to his wealth.

The other response involves giving in to the experience of the inevitable heartbreaks of life; from death, loss, separation, change, disruption, and disappointment without despair. The Bible is full of such responses to sadness. An entire devotional tradition on Mary is centered on the "seven sorrows" she experienced. It's the response of Jesus when he wept at the death of Lazarus and when he wept over the city of Jerusalem. Giving in to sadness when we experience the inevitable bitterness of life doesn't mean we lack faith, hope, and love—or joy— any more than Jesus or Mary lacked these.

Be cautious when you ask in this prayer to sow joy where there is sadness. It would be unwise to try to deprive ourselves or others of experiencing life's inevitable sadnesses in favor of a shallow "joy" that amounts to a denial of reality. We don't sow joy by denying sadness. Joy comes not by racing around or bypassing sadness, but walking through sadness. Without the experience of sadness, our joy will be shallow.

> *O Jesus, you who wept over the loss of a friend and over the city of Jerusalem, help me to sit with sadness when it comes so that I may come to know more fully the joy of your salvation. Help me, also, to learn how to be with others in their sadness so they, too, come to know your joy.*

"Grant that I may not so much seek to be consoled as to console . . ."

"CLOSURE" IS A LIFETIME
EFFORT FOR CHRISTIANS

So let us not grow weary in doing what is right, for we will reap at harvest time, if we do not give up.

Galatians 6:9

Living the Peace Prayer is difficult for us because the dominant culture has trained us to value instant results and simplistic solutions. We are to seek quick resolutions to all our problems so we can "get on with our lives," lives that from then on will presumably be problem-free. Society seems to insist that we owe it to ourselves and others to move to "closure" as quickly as possible.

But what if we are being called as Christians precisely to hold the pain and contradictions and ambiguities of troublesome problems until, through God's grace, we learn from them? Or until some other good unknown to us is accomplished through our pain and suffering? What if our lives aren't meant to be problem-free, but rather we are to move on to new and perhaps even more troublesome problems after we struggle with only modest success to resolve earlier ones?

Isn't there some practical wisdom in the cynical-sounding quip that our life (so also our Christian journey here) is essentially "one darn thing after another"?

The gospel teaches that we must work our way (painstakingly and for as long as it takes) *through* hatred to love, through injury to pardon, through doubt to faith, through despair to hope, through darkness to light, through sadness to joy. Instead, our culture tells us to sprint past these undesirable realities as quickly as we can and to move to "closure" immediately. But "closure" takes time; indeed, the gospel suggests that the struggle for "closure" is a lifetime effort.

- How patient am I with my own problems? With the problems of my family? My parish?
- Do I always try to avoid situations that might require long and painstaking attention with no immediate end in sight?

"Don't just do something, stand there!"

"So, could you not stay awake with me one hour?"

Matthew 26:40

Left to our own instincts, many of us don't naturally make good counselors. We may genuinely want to console, but we often go about it badly and can easily end up making those we're trying to console feel even worse. When others are in sorrow about a loss, a hurt, or an upsetting experience, they want someone to enter their sadness with them, to share and appreciate their sadness, to be sorrowful as they are sorrowful. The deeper the sorrow, the less there is that we can "do" and the more we need to just "be there" with them. Much as we might prefer to do something, we have to just stand there in all our helplessness!

The last thing they need at that moment is the first thing many of us usually try to do—discount or dismiss their pain, or provide an instant theoretical solution to their grief. We often want to take away their sorrow or deny it for them. To offer true consolation to someone in sorrow, we must learn to be with them and never to undervalue the comfort our empathetic presence can provide them.

Scripture affirms this notion of empathetic presence in many places, but most especially in the gospel accounts of the agony in the garden, when Jesus was in the throes of profound sorrow and dread about his upcoming Passion. In one of the most haunting questions in the Bible, Jesus asks the apostles to be with him in his sorrow: "Could you not stay awake with me one hour?"

- Do I appreciate the calling Christians have to provide consolation to one another?
- What are my strengths as a consoler? What are my weaknesses?

Preaching Always—Sometimes with Words

If we are being afflicted, it is for your consolation and salvation; if we are being consoled, it is for your consolation, which you experience when you patiently endure the same sufferings that we are also suffering.

2 Corinthians 1:6

When people face disaster, suffering, and death, how are they most likely to find genuine consolation? For many, consolation will come through others who by their loving presence can help those in crisis pray and open themselves to God. Chaplains say that what many of the dying want most from them is unhurried time to pray with them. Never underestimate the consolation such shared prayer can provide.

Shared prayer is part of the broader potential for consolation at work in such situations. We also witness to the disconsoled by our very lives that reflect, however imperfectly, the truth and power of the Christian faith.

A statement attributed to St. Francis seems apt here: We are to preach always—and sometimes with words!

In life-and-death crises, we aren't likely to provide consolation with words only. Words aren't as important as the message our life can provide to the disconsoled when they most need it. The message our presence can give to the disconsoled: "It isn't too late. As God's love is at work in the life of the one who prays with me, so God's love can be at work in mine, even now."

What gives ultimate consolation and hope to anyone facing disaster, suffering, and death is the promise that they, too, can break through to know and enjoy God's love, imperfectly now, but fully in eternity. Any consolation short of that in any dire situation is not really much consolation at all.

- Am I willing to be a witness to those who are in desperate need of consolation?
- Do I have enough confidence in God's grace to expect that others in crisis can be consoled by my presence and the witness of my faith?

"Grant that I may not so much
seek to be . . . understood as to
understand . . ."

Is it better to understand
or to be understood?

And this is my prayer: that your love may increase ever more and more in knowledge and every kind of perception. . . .

Philippians 1:9 (NAB)

How satisfying it is to be understood by others, by our family and friends and coworkers! Who of us isn't deeply gratified when we realize that others truly understand us and why we respond as we do? Who of us isn't hurt when we feel others misunderstand us or misjudge our motives?

As fulfilling as it is to be understood, it's just as richly rewarding to understand. We're rational beings, so any time we break through to learn the truth about others or gain insight into why they act the way they do, it's a satisfying experience, resembling the loving response that St. Paul describes as "rejoicing in the truth." But this isn't just an abstract conformity of our minds to reality. To understand others is to break through to them in a way that frees us from the burden of judging them, patronizing them, or trying to control them. How much wisdom there is in that old saying that to know is to forgive!

Lord, help me truly to understand others so that I am free to accept them, forgive them, and respond to them as brothers and sisters.

"Grant that I may not so much seek to be . . . loved as to love . . ."

The joy of loving

Owe no one anything, except to love one another; for the one who loves another has fulfilled the law.

Romans 13:8

No experience we can have even comes close to being loved, celebrated, and affirmed just because we are who we are. Most of us probably rarely experience so-called "unconditional love," nonetheless we deeply appreciate what love others manage to give us, limited though it be by their—and our—own human flaws.

Love somehow doesn't have to be perfect to be enough to nourish us—most of us anyway.

If few underrate the satisfaction of being loved, many fail to appreciate the joy of loving, of giving love. Because we assume that giving love is so much more difficult and less satisfying than receiving love, we don't demand or expect ourselves to become great or even good lovers. But our ability to love is precisely what reveals that we are maturing, that we are learning something about life's journey. And when we are growing into the loving Christians we are called to be, what could make us happier? What could be more satisfying?

When we pray for the grace to love, we are asking to become grown-up Christians who have learned that loving is, indeed, the richest and most personally rewarding experience available to us on this earth.

- In what ways am I stuck in the childish pattern of expecting to be loved without loving in return?
- Have I set for myself the clear goal of becoming a loving person?
- Do I appreciate that loving holds more potential for making me happy than just expecting love from others?

SEEKING TO LOVE RATHER
THAN SEEKING TO BE LOVED

*See what love the Father has given us, that we should
be called children of God; and that is what we are.*

1 John 3:1

We are always seeking to be loved because, by our
very nature, we cannot become complete persons alone.
We crave loving relationships as strongly as we crave food
and drink. So much insight into human nature is revealed
in that evocative statement in Genesis 2:18: "It is not good
for the man to be alone."

But in another sense, "seeking to be loved" is a thorny
problem. If one has been denied sufficient love during
crucial early years or if one's sense of self-worth is weak
for whatever reason, that person can easily slip into a
tormented life of "seeking to be loved" in everything. That
person becomes demanding, manipulative, cloying.
"Seeking to be loved" is like trying to satisfy an addiction,
trying to get a quick fix of love while rarely having the will
or the capacity to love others in return.

By contrast, seeking to love is a rich blessing we
would want to pray for daily. When we ask in the Peace
Prayer for the grace to love, we are asking to live fully out
of the glorious freedom of the children of God, who are

liberated from the psychological prison of having "to seek to be loved."

> *Thank you, heavenly Father, for creating me, redeeming me, and giving me the promise of eternal life—all out of your unbounded love. Help me to love as I am so wonderfully loved.*

"For it is in giving that we receive . . ."

"It is in giving that we receive"

The one who sows sparingly will also reap sparingly, and the one who sows bountifully will also reap bountifully. Each of you must give as you have made up your mind, not reluctantly or under compulsion, for God loves a cheerful giver.

2 Corinthians 9:6-7

The psychology of giving is a fascinating topic, filled with irony and paradox. We can be incredibly generous in some settings, but we can be the most tight-fisted of creatures in others settings. Our generosity can surprise even ourselves, yet at other times we find ourselves hoarding with no obvious need to do so.

It is jokingly said that we are to give until it hurts, but we can just as rightly say we are to give until it feels good. Which is more accurate? It's hard to say, because often giving of our time, talent, and treasure hurts and feels good simultaneously!

My guess is that giving satisfies a profound human need, and so giving carries within itself its own rewards.

In giving we reveal the greatest gift available to us but which is often grossly obscured, namely our true selves.

If we are, indeed, created in the image and likeness of God, how could our souls not thrill when we are responding in that most Godlike of ways, with creative, outflowing generosity? We were created to give and to share—it's in the very fiber of our being. When we ask in the Peace Prayer to be generous in giving, we are asking for the grace to respond in accordance with our truest self.

Lord, help me to give until it feels good!

WE ARE CALLED TO BE OPEN
TO BOTH GIVING AND RECEIVING

Peter said to him, "You will never wash my feet."

John 13:8

When Peter refused to let Jesus wash his feet, he was part of the old order that divided giving from receiving, slave from master, rich from poor. For Peter and his contemporaries, the world was composed of those whose destiny was to give or those whose destiny was to receive. For Jesus to sink to doing what the lowliest slaves did was unthinkable, and Peter wanted no part of it.

Jesus offers a radically different outlook. In the act of washing and when he himself received the solace of others, Jesus shows that we must be free to both give and receive at every moment, at every stage of our lives. Just as it would be fatal for the body if one could inhale but not exhale, so it is fatal to the soul if one gives without receiving or receives without giving. Giving/receiving is to the soul what breathing is to the body. We must always be ready to take and to give equally. Jesus' followers are not to think of themselves exclusively as either givers or receivers. They are part of a new creation, a new order wherein individuals are free to give and free to receive as common needs arise. The secret of life that the children of

God hold is that their hearts and minds are free to give *and* to receive, to serve *and* to be served as situations demand.

This openness to giving/receiving is what we pray for in the Peace Prayer.

- How free am I to respond to the needs of others?
- Am I more willing to give help to others than to receive help from them?

"It is in pardoning that we are pardoned . . ."

WHY PARDONING SEEMS TO
GO AGAINST THE GRAIN

"I will give you the keys of the kingdom of heaven, and whatever you bind on earth will be bound in heaven, and whatever you loose on earth will be loosed in heaven."

Matthew 16:19

One definition of pardon is "to release a person from liability for a crime or offense." This definition helps me understand why the very idea of pardoning someone who we are sure has knowingly and grievously wronged another seems troublesome.

Who are we to "release" others from what seems to be the inevitable consequences of their actions? Aren't there "laws" of human nature and social reality, the violations of which are no longer subject to "release" by anybody? Won't humans who wantonly kill or maim others solely for selfish reasons, for example, rightly come to guilt themselves and know in their heart of hearts that some punishment must be meted out? That there is a debt that must paid? Isn't the guilt of some so strong that they freely accept their punishment as the only way to rejoin the human race?

Into the playing out of this seemingly inevitable and apt process of justice, along we come and act as if we can suspend these "laws" of the moral universe by "releasing" the guilty from liability! Not only is there the question of *should* we "release" another from liability and guilt, there's the more basic question of *could* we do it. I can "release" you from the liabilities of the law of gravity all I want, but if you jump off the 20th floor you are still going to break your neck.

It is hard to escape the sense that pardoning is declaring, "This crime or offense never happened—or if it did, you weren't responsible enough to have to pay for it. There never was any debt here that anyone need worry about repaying." It's difficult to avoid the sense that pardoning involves tampering with and grossly distorting truth . . . that it amounts to fools rushing in and trying to meddle in metaphysical realities where angels dare not tread. Without the gospel, this seems to be where we get stuck.

But Jesus says we cannot judge and condemn others. We cannot ever for any reason declare them beyond our pardon, that is, we cannot declare that their actions have exiled them from the human family to such an extent that irreversible metaphysical laws now take over and pardon is irrelevant.

The radical revelation of the gospel is that we can no longer claim that any human actions set off metaphysical tripwires creating debts that must be paid and are somehow outside of our control. Or, if human acts can be said to create such debts, then these debts have somehow already been paid by the life, suffering, death, and resurrection of Jesus.

There are parables and other explicit texts in the gospels declaring the duty we have to pardon and forgive others. But we often miss the obvious implications of Matthew 16:19 and John 20:22-23 in this context. In these two texts, Jesus promises the disciples that what is bound or loosed on earth is bound or loosed "in heaven," and that sins they forgive are forgiven or sins they declared unforgiven remain unforgiven.

Could there be a clearer declaration that we humans have been given final authority to pardon others, as well as to determine how best we are to treat one another as one family under one Father? How much clearer could a text be telling us there are no blind metaphysical laws of morality we must submit to or debts that must somehow be satisfied?

Certainly, our pardon and forgiveness do not mean offenders have no price to pay if they want to take a place in the human family again. The price to be paid is the often long and painful discipline, the elusive goal of which is ending their destructive or disruptive behavior. But the offenders' discipline is not revenge, not punishment for sake of punishment, not payment of moral debts, not the balancing of some moral scale held by a goddess of justice. The goal is analogous to a medical one—to restore health so that the person can return to a normal life.

- Is learning to forgive and pardon others part of your daily prayer or spiritual discipline?
- Are there particular cases of wrongs done against you for which you are avoiding the call to forgive the wrongdoer?

My attitudes on forgiveness are hard to dislodge

"How often am I to forgive my brother if he goes on wronging me? As many as seven times?" Jesus replied, "I do not say seven times but seventy times seven."

Matthew 18:21-22 (NAB)

When I react to this passage, I seem inevitably to come away from it with a smug and self-righteous attitude to pardon and forgiveness intact. Sure, I acknowledge that this passage and many others call on me to pardon and forgive others frequently. But when I ask myself if I'm allowing the radical implications of this and other gospel passages to begin to change my mind and heart, I'm not sure I've moved off dead center.

Even when I acknowledge that I am to pardon and forgive others a virtually infinite number of times, somehow I continue to think of pardon and forgiveness as the exception rather than the rule.

Even when I acknowledge that I am to pardon and forgive others a virtually infinite number of times, I reserve the right—and regard it as my solemn duty, in fact—to try each and every case of wrongdoing in my heart, and maybe in the 489th case I've judged, I'll find sufficient grounds to withhold pardon and forgiveness.

Even when I acknowledge that I am to pardon and forgive others a virtually infinite number of times, I cling to my bias that the world is divided into good people who grant forgiveness and bad people who need forgiveness—and, of course, I know which of these two groups I'm in.

Even when I acknowledge that I am to pardon and forgive others a virtually infinite number of times, I often fail to acknowledge and act on the truth that pardoning and forgiving is at the top of the list of responses that reveal whether or not I'm trying to be a follower of Jesus.

If it did nothing else than remind us of the gospel truth that "in pardoning we are pardoned," the Peace Prayer would deserve a prominent place in our daily prayer and spiritual discipline.

Lord, I have no trouble seeing everywhere the need to forgive others. Make known to me with equal clarity my own great need for the forgiveness of others. Just as I recognize that I am called to forgive others, let me also live in expectation that others will forgive me.

A PEACEFUL GREETING SIGNALS
WILLINGNESS TO PARDON

Jesus came and stood among them and said,
"Peace be with you."

John 20:19

Here is a simple but deceptively difficult goal to strive for in our daily effort to make the Peace Prayer our own: learn to greet and welcome others always and everywhere in the same spirit of pardon and peace that the risen Christ greeted his disciples after the Resurrection.

Remember the scene. The disciples are huddled together in a locked room after the darkest days of Jesus' passion, crucifixion, and death. In addition to being fearful, confused, and despairing, they are probably not a little guilt-ridden for having abandoned him. They were probably expecting at least some mild rebuke from him. And they might even have felt a little better on a purely human level if he *had* rebuked them.

Instead, Jesus greets them with a simple, "Peace be with you." He seems to be pardoning them in such a generous way that they are even spared the shame of being reminded how badly they needed pardoning. How forgiving, loving, and liberating—how startling—such a greeting must have been to them! Not a word about the recent bitter past. No chiding, no sarcastic comments, no recriminations. No taunting reminders of how they were fair-weather friends who turned tail and ran. Bygones, it seems, aren't even worth mentioning by the risen Jesus. We're starting all over here with the help of the Holy Spirit, he seems to be saying. Peace, that's what's in our future.

Peace be with you!

"And it is in dying that
we are born to eternal life."

Praying for a "happy death"

Where, O death, is your victory?
Where, O death, is your sting?

1 Corinthians 15:55

During my childhood, we used to pray frequently at home and at church for "a happy death." I haven't heard that phrase in decades, and it has dropped out of the collections of favorite Catholic prayers published nowadays. The wonder is that we could acknowledge death so openly, frequently, and routinely in our prayer. And that we could have linked "happy" to death in the teeth of the prevailing secularistic culture where such a notion surely was as counterintuitive as asking for a "satisfying sickness."

To have prayed for a good or "peaceful" death would perhaps have softened the notion a bit—and I'm sure that, in many cases, was what we meant. Nonetheless, to ask for a "happy" demise seems almost as if we were mocking death, as if we were saying: "Hey, Death, you big bully, we're not afraid of you. With God's help, we're expecting to turn you on your head and are confident enough to use 'happy' in the same breath as you."

Praying for a happy death seems solidly Franciscan and surely wouldn't be out of place in the Peace Prayer. But the use of "dying" in the Peace Prayer is more abstract and creedal ("it is in dying that we are born to eternal life"), as if we were reminding ourselves that dying is the gateway to something new. A gate, a door, a passageway, an entrance is neither intrinsically evil nor intrinsically good. Yet inevitably and instinctively, we ascribe evil to *how* we die—it's evil if we are killed violently at the hand of another or if we are destroyed by the seemingly impersonal forces of diseases such as cancer. But have we also wrongly ascribed evil to dying itself, to *that* we die? Sometimes it seems we regard dying as so morally abhorrent to us that the only prayer we can muster is to be spared that outrage indefinitely.

"The foolish fear death as the greatest of evils," noted St. Ambrose.

Over against the only-good-death-is-no-death tendency, it might be healthy to begin once again to start praying for a "happy death." And to make St. Francis, who declared as he was dying, "Welcome, Sister Death," a special patron, sharing the role with St. Joseph, who traditionally was the patron saint for a happy death.

*Lord, only you know what will make my death happy,
and so I ask for the grace daily to entrust my death and
dying to you. Help me to trust that my death will come
whenever my life here is fulfilled, and that you alone know
when that hour comes.*

THERAPEUTIC CHATTER ABOUT
DEATH AND DYING

... so that through death he might destroy the one who has the power of death, that is, the devil, and free those who all their lives were held in slavery by the fear of death.

Hebrews 2:14-15

Talking About Death Won't Kill You is the clever title of a recently published book filled with much advice and counsel offered as therapeutic. Ironically, the book and the title is also a backhanded acknowledgment that death hasn't lost all of its taboo. Even if talking about death won't kill anybody, how can talking about it better "prepare" one for dying? "Planning" your dying may perhaps make your passing tidier and less troublesome for your family and friends. And there may be a brief stage at which one can think about dying as one's last great adventure—and so one may want to chat about it in advance the way one might talk about a trip to the Antarctic.

Yet, isn't losing control the very essence of dying? What is dying if it isn't an act of surrendering *everything*? At least being forced to experience everything being taken from you? If you in your fragile little canoe are being inexorably pulled to the very edge of Niagara Falls, wouldn't even the faintest suggestion that you could (or were obligated to) do anything to control your plunge into the abyss be so absurd as to be laughable?

The pregnant woman and her family can spend many months or years "preparing" for the baby. But what can the fetus do to "prepare"? The unborn are the very definition of helplessness. If somehow it might be theoretically possible to communicate with the unborn to try to help them "prepare" for the shock of birth, how could they understand anything? How is it possible for a fetus to become a willing and helpful partner in its own birth?

Just as birth is unknown and unknowable to the fetus, so death is unknown and unknowable to the dying. Because death is essentially unknown and unknowable, we have no choice but to approach it through some kind of faith or belief system. That in part is why contemporary Western culture, which is collectively out of the habit of responding in faith to anything, carries so much conflicted ambiguity about death and dying.

As earnestly as the prevailing culture might want to reduce death to a manageable medical or psychological problem to be solved, death remains a wild mystery untamable by even those armies of highly credentialed "counselors" that contemporary secular institutions always muster these days to help survivors get through deadly "tragedies."

And try as solemnly and reverently as religions might to put death and dying into a handy perspective, they haven't succeeded either in opening many of the secrets of death or in raising to new levels the art of dying. But at least religion has the good sense to bow ceremonially to the mystery and let silence or such sounds as the singing of a hymn, the tolling of a bell, or the soft thud of a shovelful of dirt on a casket lid do most of the "talking."

In the Peace Prayer, we are reminded that "it is in dying that we are born to eternal life." "Dying" is a form of birth. We can only "practice" going through the big, scary door of death by going through the many little doors of dying to self. These little "dyings" are, perhaps, something like inoculations—we're getting dying in a dosage we presumably can handle and that may take some of the terror out of our final passage. The "vaccination" isn't the talking, the planning, the philosophizing about and the managing of dying, but in the actual little deaths and dyings wherein silent prayer usually seems more helpful than any kind of talking.

- Is my death and dying the subject of my prayer?
- What am I asking for when I pray about my death?
- Can I willingly offer my death to God today as a way to help me prepare for dying?

"MAY YOU DIE OF AN ACUTE CASE OF LIVING"

*Therefore I will allot him a portion among the great . . .
because he poured out himself to death. . . .*

Isaiah 53:12

My entry for a Golden Well-Wish about death, for an all-purpose epitaph that in all cases might be apt, is this: "May you die of an acute case of living." Or even more basic: "May you live till you die."

May you die from living rather than die from the fear of living. May you die with your boots on, that is, in the course of living to your full measure the gifts you have and are, rather than trying to live as if the point of life was to avoid death, living without ever having put on any boots at all. Whenever or however death comes, may it come because—and after—you have lived fully the days you were given.

Between birth and death, one's history may well have many tragic episodes that could well have turned out differently, perhaps even much better than they did. But no birth or death is a "tragedy." *That* we die is no "tragedy." To think of death as a "tragedy" implies that the person died ultimately because of some personal moral failure or lapse; that had the dying only summoned up more heroic virtue, they could have avoided death altogether and literally "lived happily ever after." Just to say it this way reveals the absurdity of thinking of anyone's death as a "tragedy."

This Golden Well-Wish for any and all human death is in the spirit of the Peace Prayer, for it suggests that death and dying are functional aspects of life and living, a part of the life-death-resurrection cycle.

- What in my daily living am I most fearful of?
- What am I most fearful of when I think about dying and my own death?

"I WILL GIVE MY LIFE"

I am already being poured out as a libation, and the time of my departure has come.

2 Timothy 4:6

Much wisdom is hidden in the way we seem to have to talk about life and death. Notice, for example, how similar sounding but how radically different are these two statements:

"I will take my life."

"I will give my life."

The first sentence, inevitably and instantly, conjures up something negative, and gets our attention the way the screech of sliding fingernails down a chalkboard gets our attention. When we hear the first sentence, we assume that, out of despair or desperation, those who utter it are about to commit suicide. Further, we tend to read into the statement the implication that they are doing so because they feel compelled, they have no other choice.

The second sentence, inevitably and instantly (for me, anyway), brings to mind something positive, even heroic. A soldier volunteering for a hazardous rescue mission. A missionary heading into hostile territory where she faces possible martyrdom. Someone committing themselves to a religious life of service or teaching or prayer. Spouses vowing a lifetime of faithful devotion to one another. And in this sentence, we sense that those who utter it aren't compelled but are choosing freely.

There was an account in a secular magazine recently by a Pakistani journalist who claimed to be reporting from inside the innermost circles of a Palestinian resistance movement that recruited, trained, and supported suicide bombers. The journalist reported that one condition imposed by his sources was that the bombers had to be referred to in the article as "martyrs" because that is the way they see themselves and the way many in their culture see them.

No matter who we are or how great the desperation that might drive us to distort this knowledge, we know in our heart of hearts that life is not for the taking, but for the giving. In the Peace Prayer, we ask for the strength to say: "I will give my life."

Lord, help me each day to be ready to give my life, not only in the big and heroic ways but in all the small ways as well.

To Deny Death Is to Live Unrealistically

"Amen, amen, I say to you, unless a grain of wheat falls to the ground and dies, it remains just a grain of wheat; but if it dies, it produces much fruit."

John 12:24 (NAB)

That life comes out of death is an abstract truth that applies in some degree to all of nature. Jesus used the metaphor of seeds, which "die" and blossom into new plants. Yet we realize instantly that it's still the same kind of plant that emerges from the dead seed. So death, it turns out, is nature's way of recycling the same kind of life. The death we know doesn't bring any evolutionary leap forward, so to speak. The death we see all around us doesn't break through to supernatural life.

Christ's death and resurrection and our participation in it are about spiritual death and life. When we "die" with Christ, we don't return to the same kind of life. Rather, we become something new, a new creature, as St. Paul says. This new kind of life starts in time, but we cannot experience it fully except in eternity.

When we pray this final line of the Peace Prayer, "it is in dying that we are born to eternal life," we remind ourselves that death is the one and only door to the full flowering of our eternal life. My denial of my death is a way of living unrealistically, even ignorantly and blindly. I'd be responding much more realistically if I followed the example of St. Francis by "welcoming Sister Death" in the sense of seeing death as the gateway to new life and of befriending death as a beginning rather than fearing it as the end of me.

Which of these two approaches to death and dying seems, in the end, the most practical? The first, from poet Dylan Thomas, is one of the most famous lines of poetry in English in the last half-century. The second is the sixth verse of the hymn "All Creatures of Our God and King," inspired by a text from St. Francis (a verse, incidentally, we rarely seem to sing anymore).

Do not go gentle into that good night . . .
Rage, rage against the dying of the light.

And you, most kind and gentle death,
Waiting to hush our final breath . . .
You lead to heav'n the child of God,
Where Christ our Lord the way has trod.

We adore you, O Christ, and we praise you, because by your death on the cross and your rising from the tomb you have redeemed the world.

We don't respond from earthly motives alone

Think of what is above, not of what is on earth. For you have died, and your life is hidden with Christ in God.

Colossians 3:2-3 (NAB)

The prevailing spirit of self-giving and the words "it is in dying that we are born to eternal life" remind us that the Peace Prayer isn't a motto for social work but a call to Christian transformation. This prayer is about turning over our lives to Christ, about dying to the false self. It is about living the gospel precepts, including "what you do to the least of my brothers and sisters, you do to me." We could not long sustain a commitment to live the Peace Prayer if we are operating only out of a professional ethic of social work. Or any other human motive, however noble.

A telling story about Mother Teresa of Calcutta is the one of a business executive witnessing her personally caring for a dying man, whose body was filthy and stinking from incurable diseases. "I wouldn't do that for a million dollars," he said. "Nor would I," she responded, explaining that she didn't view such service as a *job* but as a personal religious response to Jesus.

So it is with trying to live the Peace Prayer. The self-giving it asks for is something most of us probably wouldn't do for a million dollars either—because we don't do *any* of our Christian responses for earthly motives alone, but for heavenly ones, for motives that satisfy the deepest spiritual needs in us that reveal our divine origins.

Lord, when I seem to be overwhelmed by the demands of
the Christian life, help me to clarify anew why I do things.
Help me to regain genuine Christian motives
for my responses.